Espresso And Coffee Recipes

The Ultimate Coffee And Espresso Recipes You Can Easily Make At Home

Disclaimer

All the material contained in this book is provided for educational and informational purposes only. No responsibility can be taken for any results or outcomes resulting from the use of this material.

While every attempt has been made to provide information that is both accurate and effective, the author does not assume any responsibility for the accuracy or use/misuse of this information.

Table of Contents

Introduction

The average American will drink 416 8 ounce cups of coffee in a year. Coffee is one of the most popular drinks in the world, and there is a very good reason for this. For many people coffee gives that much needed boost of energy to wake up in the mornings and of course there are other people like myself who just love how coffee tastes. Many people do not realize that there are a wide range of coffee recipes that can change your cup of coffee into another drink altogether. If you are bored of having your plain cup of coffee in the morning, there are plenty of ways you can spice up your cup of coffee, and still enjoy that boost of energy coffee give in the morning. Here are a few tips that you can try that will help make your coffee even better!

Coffee Tips

- Use a French press for more a stronger taste

- Use fresh coffee beans
- Roast your own beans for fresher tasting coffee
- Make sure that water is 195-205F when brewing coffee
- Use filtered water for better tasting coffee
- Grind your own beans

These recipes will give you a taste of some of the great coffee recipes you can make and will let you try different flavors from around the world.

Hot Buttered Toffee Coffee

Ingredients

4 ounces coffee mocha ice cream

6 ounces hot coffee

2 tablespoons butterscotch topping

2 teaspoons almond liqueur

whipped topping

1 tablespoon toffee pieces or 1 tablespoon chopped chocolate-covered english toffee bar

Directions

Spoon ice cream into a large coffee mug, pour coffee, butterscotch topping and almond liqueur over ice cream.

Garnish with a dollop of whipped cream and sprinkle of toffee chips.

Hazelnut Chocolate Black Coffee

Ingredients

10 ounces hot black coffee (freshly brewed)

1/4 teaspoon chocolate extract (or to taste)

1/4 teaspoon hazelnut extract (or to taste)

1/4 teaspoon rum extract (or to taste)

Splenda sugar substitute

Directions

Pour fresh coffee into mug.

Add the extracts and Splenda.

Coco Mocha Blend

Ingredients

2 cups milk

2 tablespoons cocoa

2 tablespoons brown sugar

1 tablespoon ground coffee

1 teaspoon vanilla extract

Directions

Heat all ingredients in a small saucepan and whisk until steaming.

Strain and pour into 2 mugs.

Traditional Turkish Coffee

Ingredients

1 cup water

1 tablespoon of extra fine ground coffee (powder consistency)

1⁄8 teaspoon ground cardamom or 1 cardamom pod

sugar (optional)

Directions

Bring water and sugar to a boil in ibrik

If you do not have an ibrik, a small saucepan will work.

Remove from heat, add coffee and cardamom.

Return saucepan to heat and allow to come to a boil.

Remove from heat when coffee foams.

Again, return to heat, allowing to foam and remove from heat.

Pour into cup, and allow to sit for a few minutes for the grounds to settle to the bottom of the cup.

Cardamom pod may be served in cup for added flavor.

Gingerbread Coffee

Ingredients

3 tablespoons coffee beans, coarse ground

1 teaspoon ground cinnamon

1⁄4 teaspoon ground nutmeg

1⁄8 teaspoon ground allspice

1⁄2 teaspoon ground ginger

1 tablespoon molasses

boiling water

milk, hot

Directions

Put all ingredients, except water and milk, into a 12 oz. press pot. Add boiling water. Stir with chopstick or handle of wooden spoon.

Put lid on pot and brew 4 minutes.

Press plunger and pour coffee into large cup.

Add hot milk to taste.

To make with drip coffee: Brew coffee and stir in spices and molasses. Strain into cup.

Peppermint Coco Coffee

Ingredients
8 ounces brewed coffee

2 tablespoons powdered cocoa mix

1⁄2 teaspoon peppermint extract

2 teaspoons sugar

2 ounces skim milk

Directions
Put all dry ingredients in bottom of mug and pour in hot coffee.

Stir to dissolve sugar and cocoa mix.

Add in extract and milk and stir again.

Brown Sugar-Caramel Latte

Ingredients

1 tablespoon brown sugar

1/4 cup half-and-half

1 tablespoon caramel ice cream topping

3/4 cup hot brewed Columbian coffee

Directions

Stir brown sugar into half-and-half until dissolved.

Whip with a milk frother or small whisk.

Pour coffee into a mug, and stir in caramel sauce until dissolved.

Pour frothed half-and-half into coffee, and serve.

Classic Instant Coffee Espresso

Ingredients

1 1⁄2 teaspoons nescafe instant coffee (or depending on taste as to how strong you like your coffee)

1⁄2 cup milk

1⁄2 cup water, plus a few drops for premixing

2 teaspoons sugar (or to taste)

cinnamon (optional)

drinking cocoa powder

Directions

Put the coffee powder and sugar in a coffee mug.

Add a few drops of water (just enough to incorporate the coffee powder in to form a thick paste) Stir vigorously with a spoon and soon you will see that the coffe and sugar form a whitish shiny paste.

Boil the milk and water together.

(if you do not like milky coffee you can boil plain water (1 cup) and add a few drops of milk just to your taste straight into the mug) Pour this from a little height into the mug so that the coffee froths up.

Sprinkle a little drinking chocolate on top for effect.

You can sprinkle some cinnamon powder on top too if you like the flavour of cinnamon.

Café Mexicano

Ingredients

1 ounce Kahlua

1⁄2 ounce brandy

1 teaspoon chocolate syrup

1 dash ground cinnamon

hot coffee

sweetened whipped cream

Directions

Place Kahlúa, brandy, chocolate syrup and cinnamon in a coffee cup or mug. Fill with hot coffee. Stir to blend. Top with sweetened whipped cream.

Espresso Nightcap with Vanilla Whipped Cream

Ingredients

Espresso Nightcap:

1 1/4 cups whole milk

1/2 cup heavy cream

1 1/4 cups espresso

1 cup amaretto liqueur

Vanilla Whipped Cream:

1/2 cup whipping cream

2 tablespoons powdered sugar

1 teaspoon pure vanilla extract

Directions

For the Espresso Nightcap: Combine the milk, heavy cream, espresso, and amaretto liqueur, in a medium saucepan. Place over low heat, stirring constantly until hot but not boiling, about 3 to 5 minutes.

For the Vanilla Cream: In a large mixing bowl, beat the cream until thick Add the powdered sugar and vanilla. Continue to beat until cream holds soft peaks.

To serve: Pour the Espresso Nightcap into 4 (8-ounce) mugs. Dollop with the Vanilla Whipped Cream and serve immediately.

Irish Coffee

Ingredients

1 sugar cube

2 ounces Irish whiskey

About 1 cup hot black coffee

Softly whipped unsweetened heavy cream, for topping

5 drops creme de menthe

Directions

Put the sugar cube into a glass coffee mug and add the whiskey. Fill the mug nearly to the top with coffee. Using a spoon, gently ladle a 3/4-inch-thick layer of cream over the top of the coffee. Garnish with the creme de menthe and serve immediately.

Butter-Rum Coffee

Ingredients
1 shot butterscotch schnapps

1 shot vanilla rum

1/2 shot Irish Cream

Coffee

Whipped topping

Directions
To a coffee mug add butterscotch schnapps, rum, Irish cream and coffee. Top with whipped topping. Serve.

Holiday Spiced Coffee

Ingredients

1 1/2 cups ground coffee

1 teaspoon pumpkin pie spice

Zest of 1/2 orange, cut into thick strips

Directions

Add the ground coffee and pumpkin pie spice to the coffee filter of a drip coffee maker. Add 6 cups of water to the machine. Add the strips of orange zest to the empty carafe.

Brew according to the manufacturer's instructions. The orange zest should stay in the carafe as the cups are filled.

Spanish Coffee

Ingredients
Vanilla bean

2 cups sugar

Wedge of lime

1 1/2 ounces orange liqueur

1/2 ounce almond liqueur (recommended: Amaretto)

1 ounce coffee liqueur

1 ounce cognac

1 1/2 cups coffee

Whipped cream

Chocolate shavings

Directions
A few days before you make the coffee, split the vanilla bean in half the long way, and place it with the sugar in a closed container. To make the coffee, warm 2 brandy snifters. Take the wedge

of lime and run it around the edge of the glass to wet the rim.

Dip it in the vanilla sugar. Pour the orange liqueur into the glasses and, one at a time, light it on fire and tilt the glass to caramelize the vanilla sugared rim.

Douse the flame with a little coffee. In a copper saucepan place the almond liqueur, cognac and coffee liqueur and warm them. Divide them between the 2 snifters then top them off with more coffee. Garnish with whipped cream, chocolate shavings and a straw.

Traditional Spiced Americano with Cinnamon Whipped Cream

Ingredients

1/2 cup water

1 cup granulated sugar

1/4 teaspoon ground allspice

1/4 teaspoon ground cinnamon, plus more for dusting

1/4 teaspoon ground ginger

1 cup brewed espresso

1 cup boiling water

1 cup heavy cream

2 tablespoons confectioners' sugar

Directions

n a small saucepan, combine water and sugar over medium heat. Bring to a boil and reduce heat to low. Add the allspice, cinnamon, and ginger to the simple syrup and simmer for 5 minutes.

Take pan off heat and set aside. To the 1 cup of brewed espresso, add 1 cup of boiling water. Pour 1/2 cup of espresso into each of 4 (6 to 8-ounce) serving cups.

Add 2 tablespoons of the spiced simple syrup to each cup and stir to combine. In a large bowl, using an electric mixer with a whisk attachment, beat the heavy cream until soft peaks form. Add the confectioners' sugar and continue to beat until stiff.

Top each cup of espresso with a dollop of whipped cream. Dust with cinnamon and serve.

English Coffee

Ingredients

1/2 oz London dry gin

1/3 oz triple sec

1/3 oz Kahlua coffee liqueur

5 oz hot black coffee

1 1/2 oz whipped cream

1 tsp triple sec

Directions

Pour coffee, gin, triple sec and kahlua into an irish coffee cup and sweeten to taste. Gently float the cream on top, add a teaspoon of triple sec, and serve.

Thai Coffee

Ingredients
6 tbsp ground coffee

1/4 tsp ground coriander

4 - 5 ground cardamom

1 tsp sugar

whipping cream

ice

Directions
Ensure your coffee beans are rich and finely grounded. Ground some whole green Cardamom Pods.

Place the coffee and spices in the filter cone of your coffee maker. Brew coffee as usual, let it cool. In a tall glass, dissolve 1 or 2 teaspoons of sugar in an ounce of the coffee (it's easier to dissolve than if you put it right over ice).

Add 5-6 ice cubes and pour coffee to within about 1 inch of the top of the glass. Rest a spoon on top of the coffee and slowly pour whipping cream into the spoon. This will make the cream float on top of the coffee rather than dispersing into it right away.

French Press Vanilla Cappuccino

Ingredients

1 cup whole milk

1 cup of your favorite, good quality, coffee beans (use 1 rounded tablespoon ground coffee per cup of coffee)

Directions

Heat milk in a medium saucepan until warmed through- but do not boil. While the milk is being heated grind the coffee beans in the coffee grinder. Add the freshly ground coffee to your French press. Add 3 1/2 cups of hot boiling water then add the lid/filter assembly. Let it steep for 3 to 4 minutes then slowly press the plunger down in a steady, even manner.

While the coffee is steeping, remove milk from heat and set on a kitchen towel on your counter top so it's on a slight angle. Set an immersion blender in the shallow end of the pot and froth the milk on high speed until the foam holds, about 2 to 3 minutes blending on high. Divide the coffee out amongst the cups and spoon the frothed milk on top of each. Serve immediately.

Cinnamon Coffee

Ingredients
Cinnamon sticks

Pot hot coffee

Whipped cream

Cinnamon, for garnish

Directions
Place 1 stick of cinnamon in each of 4 coffee cups and pour in the hot coffee. Add a dollop of whipped cream and a sprinkle of cinnamon.

Dutch Coffee

Ingredients

1 oz oude genever gin

5 oz hot black coffee

1 1/2 oz whipped cream

1 tsp sugar

Directions

Pour coffee and liquor into an irish coffee cup and sweeten to taste. Gently float the cream on top, and sprinkle with nutmeg.

Coconut Oil Coffee

Ingredients

2 cups hot coffee

2 tablespoons coconut oil

2 tablespoons unsalted butter

Directions

Blend coffee, coconut oil, and butter together in a blender until oil and butter are melted and coffee is frothy.

Classic Pumpkin Spice Latte

Ingredients

2 tablespoons canned pumpkin puree

1 teaspoon vanilla extract

2 tablespoons white sugar

1 cup milk

1/4 teaspoon pumpkin pie spice

1 (1.5 fluid ounce) jigger brewed espresso

Directions

Brew your espresso. Meanwhile, in a small saucepan, whisk together the pumpkin, vanilla, sugar, pumpkin pie spice and milk.

Warm over medium heat, whisking constantly, until hot and frothy. Do not bring to a boil. Pour the espresso into a mug and pour the pumpkin spiced milk over it.

Chilled/Iced Coffee Recipes

Iced Vanilla Creamy Caramel Coffee

Ingredients

4 cups brewed coffee (cold or room temperature)

1 cup milk

1⁄3 cup French vanilla non-dairy coffee creamer

1⁄4 cup caramel ice cream topping (or more to taste)

3 cups crushed ice

canned whipped cream (optional)

Directions

Place all ingredients into blender and blend on high until the ice is completely smooth. Pour into four glasses and top with a dollop of whipped cream.

Serve immediately.

Quick and Easy Iced Espresso

Ingredients

1 cup espresso, chilled

sparkling water

crushed ice

sugar (or Splenda as or if desired)

Directions

Pour espresso over ice in a tall glass.

Fill the remainder of the glass with mineral water.

Sweeten as and if you like.

Give a quick stir and serve.

Cinnamon and Cream Iced Coffee

Ingredients

4 cinnamon sticks

6 cups strong coffee, freshly brewed

1⁄2 cup heavy cream

sugar, to taste

crushed ice

whipped cream

cinnamon

Directions

Add cinnamon sticks to hot coffee and let stand for 1 hour, then remove cinnamon.

To coffee add sugar to taste and the heavy cream, then chill.

Pour mixture into tall glasses and fill with ice, top with whipped cream and a sprinkle of cinnamon.

Classic Unsweetened Iced Coffee

Ingredients

2 cups strong coffee

1⁄2 cup 2% low-fat milk (or regular if you prefer)

1⁄2 cup sweetened condensed milk

4 cups ice cubes

whipped cream, to garnish (optional)

Directions

Combine all the ingredients in food processor or blender.

Blend until smooth.

Top with a bit of whipped cream if you want to indulge.

Greek Iced Coffee

Ingredients

1/2 cup coffee

1/2 cup milk

2 tsp honey

Directions

Blend ingredients with 1/2 cup of ice and pour into a coffee mug.

Made in the USA
Lexington, KY
03 November 2019